Air FRYER

Quick & Easy Recipes!

Publications International, Ltd.

Microwave Cooking: Microwave ovens vary in wattage. Use the cooking times as guidelines and check for doneness before adding more time.

Let's get social!
@Publications_International
@PublicationsInternational
www.pilbooks.com

Contents

Enjoy Your Air Fryer

Do you love fried foods but try to avoid them? You no longer need to worry.

The air fryer is your answer to preparing fried foods without the extra calories, fat, or mess in the kitchen. You'll get the taste and texture of fried foods—crispy, tasty, and crunchy—that you love and crave, without the added guilt often felt when consuming them. Plus, you'll soon see how your air fryer is so easy to use, cooks food faster, and provides a no-fuss clean up.

You'll love the ability to prepare fried foods in your air fryer, but you'll also soon find that you can prepare all types of other foods, too. Make everything from appetizers to meals to sides and even desserts! You can bake in it, grill in it, steam in it, roast in it, and reheat in it.

Choose from more than 100 ideas here, or create your own.

Now get started and have fun eating and serving all those foods without the added guilt.

HELPFUL HINTS

- Read the air fryer's manufacturer's directions carefully before cooking to make sure you understand the specific features of your air fryer before starting to cook.

- Preheat your air fryer for 2 to 3 minutes before cooking.

- You can cook foods typically cooked in the oven in your air fryer. But because the air fryer is more condensed than a regular oven, it is recommended that recipes cut 25°F to 50°F off the temperature and 20% off the typical cooking times.

- Avoid having foods stick to your air fryer basket by using nonstick cooking spray or cooking on parchment paper or foil. You can also get food to brown and crisp more easily by spraying occasionally with nonstick cooking spray during the cooking process.

- Don't overfill your basket. Each air fryer differs in its basket size. Cook foods in batches as needed.

- Use toothpicks to hold food in place. You may notice that light foods may blow around from the pressure of the fan. Just be sure to secure foods in the basket to prevent this.

- Check foods while cooking by opening the air fryer basket. This will not disturb cooking times. Once you return the basket, the cooking resumes.

- Experiment with cooking times of various foods. Test foods for doneness before consuming—check meats and poultry with a meat thermometer, and use a toothpick to test muffins and cupcakes.

- Use your air fryer to cook frozen foods, too! Frozen French fries, fish sticks, chicken nuggets, individual pizzas—these all work great. Just remember to reduce cooking temperatures and times.

ESTIMATED COOKING TEMPERATURES/TIMES*

FOOD	TEMPERATURE	TIMING
Vegetables (asparagus, broccoli, corn-on-cob, green beans, mushrooms, cherry tomatoes)	390°F	5 to 6 min.
Vegetables (bell peppers, cauliflower, eggplant, onions, potatoes, zucchini)	390°F	8 to 12 min.
Chicken (bone-in)	370°F	20 to 25 min.
Chicken (boneless)	370°F	12 to 15 min.
Beef (ground beef)	370°F	15 to 17 min.
Beef (steaks, roasts)	390°F	10 to 15 min.
Pork	370°F	12 to 15 min.
Fish	390°F	10 to 12 min.
Frozen Foods	390°F	10 to 15 min.

This is just a guide. All food varies in size, weight, and texture. Be sure to test your food for preferred doneness before consuming it. Also, some foods will need to be shaken or flipped to help distribute ingredients for proper cooking.

Make note of the temperatures and times that work best for you for continued success of your air fryer.

Enjoy and have fun!

Addicting Appetizers

TOASTED RAVIOLI

makes 6 servings

1 cup all-purpose flour	1/4 teaspoon salt
2 eggs	1/2 cup grated Parmesan cheese
1/4 cup water	2 tablespoons finely chopped fresh parsley (optional)
1 cup plain dry bread crumbs	1 package (10 ounces) cheese or meat ravioli, thawed if frozen
1 teaspoon Italian seasoning	1/2 cup pasta sauce, heated
3/4 teaspoon garlic powder	

1 Place flour in shallow dish. Whisk eggs and water in another shallow dish. Combine bread crumbs, Italian seasoning, garlic powder and salt in third shallow dish. Combine Parmesan cheese and parsley, if desired, in large bowl.

2 Coat ravioli with flour. Dip in egg mixture, letting excess drip back into dish. Roll in bread crumb mixture to coat. Spray with nonstick cooking spray.

3 Preheat air fryer to 390°F. Poke holes in ravioli with toothpick.

4 Cook in batches 5 to 6 minutes, turning once, until golden brown. Add to bowl with cheese; toss to coat. Serve warm with sauce.

MOZZARELLA STICKS

makes 12 servings

¼ cup all-purpose flour

2 eggs

1 tablespoon water

1 cup plain dry bread crumbs

2 teaspoons Italian seasoning

½ teaspoon salt

½ teaspoon garlic powder

1 package (12 ounces) string cheese (12 sticks)

1 cup marinara or pizza sauce, heated

---

1 Place flour in shallow dish. Whisk eggs and water in another shallow dish. Combine bread crumbs, Italian seasoning, salt and garlic powder in third shallow dish.

2 Coat each piece of cheese with flour. Dip in egg mixture, letting excess drip back into dish. Roll in bread crumb mixture to coat. Dip again in egg mixture and roll again in bread crumb mixture. Place on baking sheet. Refrigerate until ready to cook.

3 Preheat air fryer to 370°F. Line basket with parchment paper; spray with nonstick cooking spray.

4 Cook in batches 8 to 10 minutes, shaking halfway through cooking, until golden brown. Serve with marinara sauce.

BACON-WRAPPED TERIYAKI SHRIMP

makes 6 servings

1 pound large raw shrimp, peeled and deveined (with tails on)	¼ cup teriyaki marinade 12 slices bacon, cut in half crosswise

1 Place shrimp in large resealable food storage bag. Add teriyaki marinade; seal bag and turn to coat. Marinate in refrigerator 15 to 20 minutes.

2 Remove shrimp from bag; reserve marinade. Wrap each shrimp with 1 piece bacon. Brush bacon with some of reserved marinade.

3 Preheat air fryer to 390°F. Line basket with parchment paper or foil; spray lightly with nonstick cooking spray.

4 Cook 4 to 6 minutes or until bacon is crisp and shrimp are pink and opaque.

TIP: Do not use thick-cut bacon for this recipe, because the bacon will not be completely cooked when the shrimp are cooked through.

CORN TORTILLA CHIPS
makes 3 dozen chips (about 12 servings)

6 (6-inch) corn tortillas, preferably day-old

$\frac{1}{2}$ teaspoon salt

Salsa or guacamole (optional)

1. If tortillas are fresh, let stand, uncovered, in single layer on wire rack 1 to 2 hours to dry slightly.

2. Stack tortillas; cut tortillas into six equal wedges. Spray tortillas generously with nonstick olive oil cooking spray.

3. Preheat air fryer to 370°F.

4. Cook in batches 5 to 6 minutes, shaking halfway through cooking. Sprinkle with salt. Serve with salsa or guacamole, if desired.

NOTE: Tortilla chips are served with salsa as a snack, used as the base for nachos and used as scoops for guacamole, other dips or refried beans. They are best eaten fresh, but can be stored, tightly covered, in a cool place 2 or 3 days.

CRISPY RANCH CHICKEN BITES >>

makes 6 servings

1 pound boneless skinless chicken breasts

½ cup ranch salad dressing, plus additional for serving

2 cups panko bread crumbs

1. Cut chicken into 1-inch cubes. Place ½ cup dressing in small bowl. Spread panko in shallow dish. Dip chicken in dressing; shake off excess. Roll in panko to coat. Spray chicken with nonstick cooking spray.

2. Preheat air fryer to 370°F. Line basket with parchment paper.

3. Cook in batches 8 to 10 minutes or until golden brown and cooked through. Serve with additional ranch dressing.

SAVORY PITA CHIPS

makes 4 servings

2 whole wheat or white pita bread rounds

2 tablespoons grated Parmesan cheese

1 teaspoon dried basil

¼ teaspoon garlic powder

1. Carefully cut each pita round in half horizontally; split into two rounds. Cut each round into six wedges. Spray wedges with nonstick cooking spray.

2. Combine Parmesan cheese, basil and garlic powder in small bowl; sprinkle evenly over pita wedges.

3. Preheat air fryer to 350°F.

4. Cook 8 to 10 minutes, shaking occasionally during cooking, until golden brown. Cool completely.

CINNAMON CRISPS: Substitute butter-flavored cooking spray for nonstick cooking spray and 1 tablespoon sugar mixed with ¼ teaspoon ground cinnamon for Parmesan cheese, basil and garlic powder.

PIGGIES IN A BASKET >>

makes 4 servings

1 package (8 ounces) refrigerated crescent roll dough	1 package (about 12 ounces) cocktail franks

1. Cut crescent dough into strips. Wrap dough around each frank.
2. Preheat air fryer to 350°F.
3. Cook in batches 3 to 4 minutes or until golden brown.

HAPPY APPLE SALSA WITH CINNAMON PITA CHIPS

makes 3 servings

2 teaspoons sugar	1 tablespoon finely diced celery
1/4 teaspoon ground cinnamon	1 tablespoon finely diced carrot
2 pita bread rounds, split	1 tablespoon golden raisins
1 tablespoon jelly or jam	1 teaspoon lemon juice
1 medium apple, diced	

1. Combine sugar and cinnamon in small bowl. Cut pita rounds into wedges. Spray with nonstick cooking spray; sprinkle with cinnamon-sugar.
2. Preheat air fryer to 350°F.
3. Cook 8 to 10 minutes, shaking occasionally, until lightly browned. Set aside to cool.
4. Meanwhile, place jelly in medium microwavable bowl; microwave on HIGH 10 seconds. Stir in apple, celery, carrot, raisins and lemon juice. Serve salsa with pita chips.

CAPRESE-STYLE TARTLETS

makes 6 tartlets

---

3 tomatoes, cut into 4 slices each

3 tablespoons prepared pesto

1 sheet frozen puff pastry (half of 17¼-ounce package)

6 ounces fresh mozzarella cheese

2 tablespoons chopped kalamata olives

---

1 Place tomatoes in large resealable food storage bag. Add pesto; toss to coat. Marinate at room temperature 30 minutes.

2 Unfold puff pastry; thaw 20 minutes on lightly floured surface.

3 Preheat air fryer to 370°F. Line basket with parchment paper.

4 Cut out six (4-inch) rounds from pastry. Top each round with 2 tomato slices. Cook in batches 8 to 10 minutes or until pastry is light golden and puffed.

5 Cut cheese into six (¼-inch-thick) slices. Top each tart with 1 cheese slice. Cook in batches 1 minute or until cheese is melted. Top tarts evenly with olives. Serve warm.

LAVASH CHIPS WITH ARTICHOKE PESTO

makes 1½ cups pesto (about 8 servings)

3 pieces lavash bread

¼ cup plus 2 tablespoons olive oil, divided

¾ teaspoon kosher salt, divided

1 can (14 ounces) artichoke hearts, rinsed and drained

½ cup chopped walnuts, toasted*

¼ cup packed fresh basil leaves

1 clove garlic, minced

2 tablespoons lemon juice

¼ cup grated Parmesan cheese

*To toast nuts, cook in preheated 325°F parchment paper-lined air fryer 3 to 4 minutes or until golden brown.

1 Preheat air fryer to 370°F. Line basket with parchment paper.

2 Brush both sides of lavash with 2 tablespoons oil. Sprinkle with ¼ teaspoon salt. Cut to fit in air fryer, if necessary. Cook in batches 6 to 8 minutes, shaking occasionally, until lavash is crisp and browned. Cool on wire rack.

3 Place artichoke hearts, walnuts, basil, garlic, lemon juice and remaining ½ teaspoon salt in food processor; pulse about 12 times until coarsely chopped. While food processor is running, slowly stream remaining ¼ cup oil until smooth. Add Parmesan cheese and pulse until blended.

4 Serve lavash with pesto.

NOTE: You can also toast walnuts in preheated 350°F oven 6 to 8 minutes, if preferred.

GREEN BEAN DIPPERS >>

makes 6 servings

1 egg	1 tablespoon olive oil
1 pound green beans, ends trimmed	½ teaspoon garlic powder
½ cup plain dry bread crumbs	¼ teaspoon salt
2 tablespoons grated Parmesan cheese	Prepared salad dressing (optional)

1 Whisk egg in large bowl. Add green beans; toss to coat. Combine bread crumbs, Parmesan cheese, oil, garlic powder and salt in small bowl. Sprinkle bread crumb mixture over green beans.

2 Preheat air fryer to 390°F. Line basket with parchment paper.

3 Cook in batches 8 to 10 minutes, shaking occasionally during cooking, until crispy. Serve with dressing, if desired.

MINI CHICKPEA CAKES

makes 2 dozen cakes (about 8 servings)

1 can (about 15 ounces) chickpeas, rinsed and drained	¼ cup creamy Italian salad dressing, plus additional for dipping
1 cup grated carrots	1 egg
⅓ cup seasoned dry bread crumbs	

1 Coarsely mash chickpeas in medium bowl with fork or potato masher. Stir in carrots, bread crumbs, ¼ cup salad dressing and egg; mix well.

2 Shape chickpea mixture into 24 patties, using about 1 tablespoon mixture for each.

3 Preheat air fryer to 370°F. Spray basket with nonstick cooking spray.

4 Cook in batches 10 minutes, turning halfway through cooking, until lightly browned. Serve warm with additional salad dressing for dipping, if desired.

THE BIG ONION

makes 6 servings

DIPPING SAUCE

- ½ cup light mayonnaise
- 2 tablespoons horseradish
- 1 tablespoon ketchup
- ¼ teaspoon paprika
- ⅛ teaspoon salt
- ⅛ teaspoon ground red pepper
- ⅛ teaspoon dried oregano

ONION

- 1 large sweet onion (about 1 pound)
- ½ cup all-purpose flour
- 1 tablespoon buttermilk
- 2 eggs
- ½ cup panko bread crumbs
- 1 tablespoon paprika
- 1½ teaspoons seafood seasoning

1. For sauce, combine mayonnaise, horseradish, ketchup, ¼ teaspoon paprika, salt, ground red pepper and oregano in small bowl; mix well. Cover and refrigerate until ready to serve.

2. For onion, cut about ½ inch off top of onion and peel off papery skin. Place onion, cut side down, on cutting board. Starting ½ inch from root, use large sharp knife to make one slice almost down to cutting board. Repeat slicing all the way around onion to make 12 to 16 evenly spaced cuts. Turn onion over; gently separate outer pieces.

3. Meanwhile, put flour in large bowl. Whisk buttermilk and eggs in another large bowl. Combine panko, 1 tablespoon paprika and seafood seasoning in another bowl.

4. Coat onion with flour, shaking off any excess. Dip entire onion in egg mixture, letting excess drip back into bowl. Then coat evenly with panko.

5. Preheat air fryer to 390°F. Spray basket with nonstick cooking spray.

6. Cook 10 to 12 minutes or until golden brown and crispy. Serve immediately with dipping sauce.

AIR-FRIED PARMESAN PICKLE CHIPS

makes 8 servings

4 large whole dill pickles
1/2 cup all-purpose flour
1/2 teaspoon salt
2 eggs

1/2 cup panko bread crumbs
2 tablespoons grated Parmesan cheese
1/2 cup garlic aioli mayonnaise or ranch dressing

1   Line baking sheet with paper towels. Slice pickles diagonally into 1/4-inch slices, place on prepared baking sheet. Pat dry on top with paper towels to remove any moisture from pickles.

2   Combine flour and salt in shallow dish. Beat eggs in another shallow dish. Combine panko and Parmesan cheese in third shallow dish.

3   Coat pickles in flour. Dip in eggs, letting excess drip back into dish, then coat evenly with panko.

4   Preheat air fryer to 390°F. Cook in batches 8 to 10 minutes or until golden brown. Remove carefully. Serve with aioli or dressing.

MINI PEPPER NACHOS

makes 40 pepper halves (2 per serving)

1 cup frozen corn, thawed

1 can (about 15 ounces) black beans, rinsed and drained

½ cup chopped tomatoes

½ teaspoon salt

20 mini sweet peppers, assorted colors, cut in half lengthwise and seeded

½ cup (2 ounces) shredded Mexican-style taco shredded cheese

½ cup sour cream (optional)

1 small avocado, chopped (optional)

2 tablespoons chopped green onion or cilantro (optional)

1 Combine corn, beans, tomatoes and salt in medium bowl. Fill peppers with about 1 tablespoon mixture. Sprinkle with cheese.

2 Preheat air fryer to 370°F. Line basket with foil. Cook peppers 5 to 7 minutes or until cheese is lightly browned and melted. Remove to serving plate.

3 Top with sour cream, avocado and green onion, if desired.

EVERYTHING SEASONING DIP WITH BAGEL CHIPS >>

makes 2 cups dip (about 16 servings)

2 large bagels, sliced vertically into rounds

1 container (12 ounces) whipped cream cheese

1½ tablespoons green onion, finely chopped (green part only)

1 teaspoon dried minced onion

1 teaspoon granulated garlic

1 teaspoon sesame seeds

1 teaspoon poppy seeds

¼ teaspoon kosher salt

1 Preheat air fryer to 350°F.

2 Coat bagel rounds generously with butter-flavored nonstick cooking spray. Cook 7 to 8 minutes, shaking occasionally, until golden brown.

3 Meanwhile, combine cream cheese, green onion, minced onion, garlic, sesame seeds, poppy seeds and salt in medium bowl until well blended.

4 Serve chips with dip.

ROSEMARY-SCENTED NUTS

makes 16 servings

1 tablespoon unsalted butter, melted

1 cup pecan halves

½ cup unsalted macadamia nuts

½ cup walnuts

½ teaspoon dried rosemary

¼ teaspoon salt

⅛ teaspoon red pepper flakes

1 Preheat air fryer to 330°F.

2 Combine butter, pecans, macadamias and walnuts in large bowl; mix well. Add rosemary, salt and red pepper flakes; stir.

3 Cook 15 to 18 minutes, shaking several times during cooking. Cool completely. Store in airtight container.

WARM GOAT CHEESE ROUNDS

makes 4 servings

1 package (4 ounces) garlic herb
  goat cheese

1 egg

1 tablespoon water

1/3 cup seasoned dry bread crumbs

Marinara sauce

1 Cut cheese crosswise into eight slices. (If cheese is too difficult to slice, shape scant tablespoonfuls of cheese into balls and flatten into 1/4-inch-thick rounds.)

2 Beat egg and water in small bowl. Place bread crumbs in shallow dish. Dip cheese rounds into egg mixture, then in bread crumbs, turning to coat all sides. Gently press bread crumbs to adhere. Place coated rounds on plate; freeze 10 minutes.

3 Preheat air fryer to 370°F. Cook in batches 10 minutes, flipping halfway through cooking, until golden brown. Serve immediately with marinara sauce.

GARLIC BITES

makes 24 bites (about 12 servings)

½ of 16-ounce package frozen phyllo dough, thawed to room temperature

¾ cup (1½ sticks) butter, melted

3 large heads garlic, separated into cloves, peeled

½ cup finely chopped walnuts

1 cup Italian-style bread crumbs

1 Remove phyllo from package; unroll and place on large sheet of waxed paper. Cut phyllo crosswise into 2-inch-wide strips. Cover phyllo with large sheet of plastic wrap and damp, clean kitchen towel. (Phyllo dries out quickly if not covered.)

2 Lay 1 strip of phyllo at a time on flat surface; brush immediately with butter. Place 1 clove of garlic at end. Sprinkle 1 teaspoon walnuts along length of strip.

3 Roll up garlic clove and walnuts in strip, tucking in side edges as you roll. Brush with butter; roll in bread crumbs. Repeat with remaining phyllo, garlic, walnuts, butter and bread crumbs.

4 Preheat air fryer to 350°F. Line basket with parchment paper. Cook in batches 6 to 8 minutes or until golden brown. Cool slightly.

FALAFEL NUGGETS

makes 12 servings

SAUCE

2½ cups tomato sauce

⅓ cup tomato paste

2 tablespoons lemon juice

2 teaspoons sugar

1 teaspoon onion powder

½ teaspoon salt

FALAFEL

2 cans (about 15 ounces each) chickpeas, rinsed and drained

½ cup all-purpose flour

½ cup chopped fresh parsley

1 egg

¼ cup minced onion

3 tablespoons lemon juice

2 tablespoons minced garlic

2 teaspoons ground cumin

½ teaspoon salt

½ teaspoon ground red pepper *or* red pepper flakes

1   For sauce, combine tomato sauce, tomato paste, 2 tablespoons lemon juice, sugar, onion powder and ½ teaspoon salt in medium saucepan. Simmer over medium-low heat 20 minutes or until heated through. Cover and keep warm until ready to serve.

2   For falafel, combine chickpeas, flour, parsley, egg, minced onion, 3 tablespoons lemon juice, garlic, cumin, ½ teaspoon salt and ground red pepper in food processor or blender; process until well blended. Shape mixture into 1-inch balls. Spray with nonstick cooking spray.

3   Preheat air fryer to 390°F. Line basket with foil; spray with cooking spray.

4   Cook in batches 12 to 15 minutes, turning halfway through cooking, until browned. Serve with sauce.

BAKED ORANGE BRIE APPETIZER

makes 6 servings

1 sheet puff pastry (half of 17¼-ounce package), thawed

⅓ cup orange marmalade

2 tablespoons chopped pecans (optional)

1 round (8 ounces) Brie cheese

1 egg white, beaten

1. Roll out puff pastry to 12-inch square. Use knife to cut off four corners; set aside scraps.

2. Spread marmalade over center of pastry to 1 inch of edges. Sprinkle pecans over marmalade, if desired. Place Brie in center on top of pecans. Brush exposed dough with egg white.

3. Gather up edges of puff pastry and bring together over center of Brie, covering cheese entirely. Pinch and twist pastry edges together to seal. Use dough scraps to decorate top of Brie. Brush lightly with egg white.

4. Preheat air fryer to 370°F.

5. Cook 8 to 10 minutes or until golden brown. Serve warm.

Best-Ever Breakfasts

HOMEMADE AIR-FRIED BAGELS

makes 4 servings

1 cup self-rising flour
1 cup plain nonfat Greek yogurt
1 large egg, beaten

Sesame seeds, poppy seeds,
    dried onion flakes, everything
    bagel seasoning (optional)
Cream cheese or butter (optional)

1 Combine flour and yogurt in bowl of electric stand mixer with dough hook*. Beat 2 to 3 minutes or until mixture is well combined. Place dough on lightly floured surface; knead by hand about 4 to 5 minutes or until dough is smooth and elastic. Form dough into a ball.

2 Cut into four equal portions. Roll each into a ball. Pull and stretch dough to create desired shape, inserting finger into center to create hole. Repeat with remaining dough.

3 Preheat air fryer to 330°F. Line basket with parchment paper. Place bagels on parchment; brush with egg wash. Sprinkle with desired toppings. Cook 8 to 10 minutes or until lightly browned.

4 Serve with cream cheese or butter, if desired.

*Or, use heavy spatula in large bowl to combine mixture.

BREAKFAST FLATS

makes 4 servings

---

1 package (about 14 ounces) refrigerated pizza dough

1½ cups (6 ounces) shredded Cheddar cheese

8 slices bacon, crisp-cooked and diced (optional)

4 eggs, fried

Kosher salt and black pepper (optional)

---

1 Divide pizza dough into four equal portions. Roll out on lightly floured surface into rectangles roughly 8½×4 inches. Top each evenly with cheese and bacon, if desired.

2 Preheat air fryer to 370°F. Line basket with parchment paper.

3 Cook in batches 5 to 7 minutes or until crust is golden brown and crisp and cheese is melted.

4 Top baked flats with fried egg; season with salt and pepper, if desired. Serve warm.

BISCUIT-WRAPPED SAUSAGES >>

makes 6 servings

1 package (8 ounces) refrigerated crescent dough sheet	1 package (about 12 ounces) fully cooked breakfast sausage links
	Maple syrup (optional)

1 Unroll crescent dough; cut dough into thin strips. Wrap each sausage link with dough. Insert wooden skewers* through sausages.

2 Preheat air fryer to 370°F.

3 Cook 5 to 7 minutes or until golden brown. Cool slightly; remove to large serving platter. Serve with maple syrup for dipping.

*Soak wooden skewers 20 minutes in cool water. Depending on the size of your air fryer, you may need to shorten the skewers to fit.

CINNAMINI BUNS

makes 2 dozen

2 tablespoons packed brown sugar	1 tablespoon butter, melted
1/2 teaspoon ground cinnamon	1/2 cup powdered sugar
1 package (8 ounces) refrigerated crescent roll dough	1 to 1 1/2 tablespoons milk

1 Combine brown sugar and cinnamon in small bowl; mix well.

2 Unroll dough and separate into two (12×4-inch) rectangles; firmly press perforations to seal. Brush dough with butter; sprinkle with brown sugar mixture. Starting with long side, roll up tightly jelly-roll style; pinch seams to seal. Cut each roll crosswise into 12 (1-inch) slices with serrated knife.

3 Preheat air fryer to 370°F. Line basket with parchment paper.

4 Cook, seam side up, in batches 5 to 7 minutes or until golden brown. Remove to wire rack; cool.

5 Combine powdered sugar and 1 tablespoon milk in small bowl; whisk until smooth. Add additional milk, 1 teaspoon at a time, to reach desired glaze consistency. Drizzle glaze over buns.

BREAKFAST PEPPERONI FLATBREAD >>

makes 2 servings

---

1 flatbread

½ cup (2 ounces) shredded mozzarella cheese

1 plum tomato, diced

12 slices turkey pepperoni, cut into quarters

1 teaspoon grated Parmesan cheese

¼ cup chopped fresh basil

---

1. Preheat air fryer to 370°F.

2. Place flatbread on parchment paper. Sprinkle with mozzarella cheese, tomatoes, pepperoni and Parmesan cheese.

3. Cook 3 to 5 minutes or until cheese is melted. Sprinkle with basil. Cool slightly before cutting.

CRUNCHY FRENCH TOAST STICKS

makes 6 servings

---

6 slices Italian bread (each 1 inch thick, about 3½ to 4 inches in diameter)

4 cups cornflake cereal, crushed

3 eggs

⅔ cup reduced-fat (2%) milk

1 tablespoon sugar

1 teaspoon vanilla

1 teaspoon ground cinnamon, plus additional for serving

¼ teaspoon ground nutmeg

1 container (6 ounces) vanilla yogurt

¼ cup maple syrup

---

1. Remove crusts from bread, if desired. Cut each bread slice into three strips. Place cornflake crumbs on waxed paper.

2. Whisk eggs, milk, sugar, vanilla, 1 teaspoon cinnamon and nutmeg in shallow dish. Dip bread strips in egg mixture, turning to generously coat all sides. Roll in cornflakes, coating all sides.

3. Preheat air fryer to 370°F. Cook in batches 8 to 10 minutes, turning halfway through cooking or until golden brown.

4. Meanwhile, combine yogurt and maple syrup in small bowl. Sprinkle with additional cinnamon, if desired. Serve French toast sticks with yogurt mixture.

OMELET CROISSANTS

makes 2 servings

2 large croissants

2 large eggs

¼ cup chopped mushrooms

¼ tablespoon chopped red and/or green bell pepper

Pinch of salt and black pepper

¼ cup (1 ounce) shredded Cheddar cheese

1 Cut slit across top of each croissant; using hands break open to separate.

2 Whisk eggs in small bowl. Add mushrooms, bell pepper, salt and black pepper. Spoon mixture equally in croissant opening. Sprinkle cheese over top.

3 Preheat air fryer to 330°F. Place croissants in parchment paper-lined basket.

4 Cook 12 to 15 minutes or until croissants are browned and eggs are set.

MAKE AHEAD: Prepared croissants can be stored in refrigerator for up to 3 days or in freezer for 1 month.

CAULIFLOWER "HASH BROWN" PATTIES

makes 8 servings

---

4 slices bacon

1 package (about 12 ounces) cauliflower rice

½ cup finely chopped onion

½ cup finely chopped red and/or green bell pepper

1 large egg

⅓ cup all-purpose flour

½ cup (2 ounces) shredded Cheddar cheese

1 tablespoon chopped fresh chives

1 teaspoon salt

½ teaspoon black pepper

---

1 Preheat air fryer to 400°F. Cook bacon 8 to 10 minutes. Remove from basket to paper towels; blot any grease from bacon. Crumble into small pieces.

2 Place cauliflower in large bowl. Add bacon, onion, bell pepper, egg, flour, cheese, chives, salt and black pepper; mix well. Shape mixture into patties; place on baking sheet. Freeze 30 minutes.

3 Preheat air fryer to 370°F. Spray basket with nonstick cooking spray. Cook 12 to 15 minutes or until browned.

AIR-FRIED OMELET SCRAMBLE

makes 2 servings

2 large eggs
2 tablespoons milk
¼ teaspoon salt
⅛ teaspoon black pepper

2 tablespoons chopped red and/or green bell pepper
2 tablespoons chopped onion
¼ cup (1 ounce) shredded Cheddar cheese, divided

1 Spray 6×3-inch baking dish or 2 small ramekins* with nonstick cooking spray.

2 Whisk eggs, milk, salt and black pepper in medium bowl. Add bell pepper, onion and 2 tablespoons cheese. Pour into prepared dish.

3 Preheat air fryer to 350°F. Cook 10 to 12 minutes, slightly breaking up eggs after 5 minutes. Top with remaining cheese.

*Depending on the size of your air fryer, you may need to modify the size of the baking dish.

WHOLE GRAIN FRENCH TOAST

makes 4 servings

½ cup egg substitute *or* 2 egg whites

¼ cup low-fat (1%) milk

½ teaspoon ground cinnamon

¼ teaspoon ground nutmeg

8 slices 100% whole wheat or multigrain bread

⅓ cup pure maple syrup

1 cup fresh blueberries

2 teaspoons powdered sugar

---

1 Preheat air fryer to 370°F. Spray basket with nonstick cooking spray.

2 Whisk egg substitute, milk, cinnamon and nutmeg in shallow bowl until well blended. Working with two slices at a time, dip each bread slice in milk mixture, turning to coat both sides; let excess mixture drip back into bowl.

3 Cook in batches 5 to 7 minutes or until golden brown, flipping halfway during cooking.

4 Microwave maple syrup in small microwavable bowl on HIGH 30 seconds or until bubbly. Stir in blueberries. Serve French toast with blueberry mixture; sprinkle with powdered sugar.

EASY RASPBERRY-PEACH DANISH

makes 8 servings

1 package (8 ounces) refrigerated crescent dough sheet

1/4 cup raspberry fruit spread

1 can (about 15 ounces) sliced peaches in juice, drained and chopped

1 egg white, beaten

1/2 cup powdered sugar

2 to 3 teaspoons orange juice

1/4 cup chopped pecans, toasted*

*To toast nuts, cook in preheated 325°F parchment paper-lined air fryer 3 to 4 minutes or until golden brown.

1 Place dough on lightly floured surface; cut in half. Roll each half into 12×8-inch rectangle.

2 Spread half of raspberry spread along center of each dough rectangle; top with peaches. Make 2-inch-long cuts from edges towards filling on long sides of each dough rectangle at 1-inch intervals. Fold strips of dough over filling. Brush with egg white.

3 Preheat air fryer to 370°F. Line basket with parchment paper. Cook each half 5 to 7 minutes or until golden brown. Remove to wire rack; cool slightly.

4 Combine powdered sugar and enough orange juice in small bowl to make pourable glaze. Drizzle glaze over danish; sprinkle with pecans.

STRAWBERRY CINNAMON FRENCH TOAST

makes 4 servings

---

1 egg

¼ cup fat-free (skim) milk

½ teaspoon vanilla

4 (1-inch-thick) diagonally-cut slices French bread (about 1 ounce each)

2 teaspoons reduced-fat margarine, softened

2 packets sugar substitute*

¼ teaspoon ground cinnamon

1 cup sliced fresh strawberries

This recipe was tested with sucralose-based sugar substitute.

---

1 Preheat air fryer to 370°F. Spray basket with nonstick cooking spray.

2 Beat egg, milk and vanilla in shallow dish or pie plate. Lightly dip bread slices in egg mixture, coating completely.

3 Cook in batches 8 to 10 minutes or until golden brown, turning halfway through cooking time.

4 Meanwhile, combine margarine, sugar substitute and cinnamon in small bowl; stir until well blended. Spread mixture evenly over French toast; top with strawberries.

APPLE BUTTER ROLLS

makes 12 servings

1 package (about 11 ounces) refrigerated breadstick dough (12 breadsticks)

2 tablespoons apple butter

1/4 cup sifted powdered sugar

1 to 1 1/2 teaspoons orange juice

1/4 teaspoon grated orange peel (optional)

1 Unroll breadstick dough; separate into 12 pieces along perforations. Gently stretch each piece to 9 inches in length. Twist ends of each piece in opposite directions three or four times. Coil each twisted strip into snail shape; tuck ends underneath. Use thumb to make small indentation in center of each breadstick coil. Spoon about 1/2 teaspoon apple butter into each indentation.

2 Preheat air fryer to 370°F. Line basket with parchment paper; spray with nonstick cooking spray.

3 Cook in batches 8 to 10 minutes or until golden brown. Remove to wire rack; cool 10 minutes.

4 Meanwhile, combine powdered sugar and 1 teaspoon orange juice in small bowl; whisk until smooth. Add additional orange juice, if necessary, to make pourable glaze. Stir in orange peel, if desired. Drizzle glaze over rolls. Serve warm.

Simple Sandwiches

VEGETABLE & CHEESE SANDWICHES

makes 2 servings

1 large zucchini, cut lengthwise into eight ¼-inch slices

2 slices sweet onion (such as Vidalia or Walla Walla), cut ¼ inch thick

1 yellow bell pepper, cut lengthwise into quarters

4 tablespoons light Caesar salad dressing, divided

4 slices sourdough bread

2 slices (1 ounce each) Muenster cheese

1 Combine zucchini, onion and bell pepper with 2 tablespoons dressing in medium bowl; toss well.

2 Preheat air fryer to 370°F. Spray basket with nonstick cooking spray.

3 Cook vegetables 6 to 8 minutes or until tender and browned. Remove from basket.

4 Brush both sides of bread lightly with remaining 2 tablespoons dressing. Cook bread in batches 2 minutes or until lightly browned. Top 2 slices bread with 2 slices cheese.

5 Arrange vegetables over cheese side of bread; top with remaining bread. Cook 1 minute or until cheese is slightly melted.

SERVING SUGGESTION: Serve with potato chips and a fresh fruit salad.

GREEK CHICKEN BURGERS WITH CUCUMBER YOGURT SAUCE

makes 4 servings

½ cup plus 2 tablespoons plain nonfat Greek yogurt

½ medium cucumber, peeled, seeded and finely chopped

Juice of ½ lemon

3 cloves garlic, minced and divided

2 teaspoons finely chopped fresh mint *or* ½ teaspoon dried mint

⅛ teaspoon salt

⅛ teaspoon ground white pepper

BURGERS

1 pound ground chicken breast

3 ounces reduced-fat crumbled feta cheese

4 large kalamata olives, rinsed, patted dry and minced

1 egg

½ to 1 teaspoon dried oregano

¼ teaspoon black pepper

Mixed baby lettuce (optional)

Fresh mint leaves (optional)

1. Combine yogurt, cucumber, lemon juice, 2 cloves garlic, 2 teaspoons chopped mint, salt and white pepper in medium bowl; mix well. Cover and refrigerate until ready to serve.

2. For burgers, combine chicken, feta cheese, olives, egg, oregano, black pepper and remaining 1 clove garlic in large bowl; mix well. Shape mixture into four patties.

3. Preheat air fryer to 370°F. Spray basket with nonstick cooking spray. Cook 12 to 15 minutes or until cooked through (165°F).

4. Serve burgers with sauce and mixed greens, if desired. Garnish with mint leaves.

CAPRESE PORTOBELLOS
makes 4 servings

2 tablespoons butter

½ teaspoon minced garlic

1 teaspoon dried parsley flakes

4 portobello mushrooms, stems removed

1 cup (4 ounces) shredded part-skim mozzarella cheese

1 cup cherry or grape tomatoes, thinly sliced

2 tablespoons fresh basil, thinly sliced

Balsamic glaze

1 Combine butter, garlic and parsley flakes in small microwavable dish. Microwave on LOW (30%) 30 seconds or until melted.

2 Wash mushrooms thoroughly; dry on paper towels. Brush both sides of mushrooms with butter mixture.

3 Preheat air fryer to 390°F. Spray basket with nonstick cooking spray.

4 Fill mushroom caps with about ¼ cup cheese each. Top with tomatoes. Cook 5 to 7 minutes or until cheese is melted and lightly browned. Top with basil.

5 Drizzle with balsamic glaze before serving.

BACON-TOMATO GRILLED CHEESE

makes 2 servings

4 slices bacon, cut in half

2 slices sharp Cheddar cheese

2 slices Gouda cheese

2 slices tomato

4 slices whole wheat or white bread

1 Preheat air fryer to 400°F. Cook bacon 8 to 10 minutes. Remove from basket to paper towels; blot any grease from bacon.

2 Meanwhile, layer 1 slice Cheddar cheese, 1 slice Gouda cheese, 1 slice tomato and 2 slices bacon between 2 bread slices. Repeat with remaining ingredients.

3 Reduce heat on air fryer to 350°F. Cook 3 to 5 minutes or until cheese is melted and bread is golden brown.

AIR-FRIED PEPPERONI PIZZA BAGELS >>

makes 4 servings

4 Homemade Air-Fried Bagels (recipe on page 44) or store bought bagels

¼ cup marinara sauce

¼ cup mini pepperoni slices

¼ cup (1 ounce) shredded mozzarella cheese

Dried oregano

1 Cut bagels in half lengthwise. Top each half with equal amount sauce, pepperoni and cheese.

2 Preheat air fryer to 350°F. Line basket with foil or parchment paper. Cook 3 to 5 minutes or until cheese is melted and browned. Sprinkle with oregano.

GRILLED CHEESE KABOBS

makes 12 servings

8 thick slices whole wheat bread

3 thick slices sharp Cheddar cheese

3 thick slices Monterey Jack or Colby Jack cheese

2 tablespoons butter, melted

1 Cut each slice bread into 1-inch squares. Cut each slice cheese into 1-inch squares. Make small sandwiches with one square of bread and one square of each type of cheese. Top with second square of bread. Brush sandwiches with butter.

2 Preheat air fryer to 370°F. Cook sandwich squares 30 seconds to 1 minute or until golden brown and cheese is slightly melted.

3 Place sandwiches on the ends of short wooden skewers, if desired, or eat as finger food.

TASTY TURKEY TURNOVERS

makes 6 servings

---

1 package (about 8 ounces) refrigerated crescent roll sheet

2 tablespoons honey mustard, plus additional for serving

3 ounces thinly sliced lean deli turkey breast

¾ cup packaged broccoli coleslaw mix

1 egg white, beaten

---

1. Roll out dough onto lightly floured surface. Using a wide glass or cookie cutter, cut into 3½-inch circles. Spread 2 tablespoons honey mustard lightly over dough circles; top with turkey and coleslaw mix. Brush edges of dough with beaten egg white. Fold circles in half; press edges with tines of fork to seal. Brush with egg white.

2. Preheat air fryer to 370°F. Spray basket with nonstick cooking spray.

3. Cook in batches 6 to 7 minutes or until golden brown. Let stand 5 minutes before serving. Serve warm or at room temperature with additional honey mustard for dipping, if desired.

CLASSIC GRILLED CHEESE >>

makes 2 sandwiches

4 slices (about $^3/_4$ ounce each) American cheese	4 slices white bread Butter, melted

1 Place 2 slices cheese each on 2 bread slices; top with remaining bread slices. Brush outsides of sandwiches with butter.

2 Preheat air fryer to 350°F. Cook in batches 3 to 5 minutes per side or until cheese melts and sandwiches are golden brown.

EASY TERIYAKI BURGERS

makes 6 servings

1 pound lean ground beef	$^1/_2$ teaspoon black pepper
$^1/_2$ cup plain dry bread crumbs	6 Kaiser rolls or hamburger buns, warmed
$^1/_4$ cup low-sodium ketchup	6 leaves green leaf lettuce
2 tablespoons low-sodium teriyaki sauce	6 slices tomato

1 Combine beef, bread crumbs, ketchup, teriyaki sauce and pepper in large bowl; mix well. Shape beef into six ($^1/_2$-inch-thick) patties.

2 Preheat air fryer to 370°F.

3 Cook in batches 8 to 10 minutes, flipping halfway through cooking, until desired doneness. Place patties on rolls. Serve with lettuce and tomato slices.

BAKED SALAMI

makes 5 servings

---

1 all-beef kosher salami (14 to 16 ounces)

½ cup apricot preserves

1 tablespoon hot pepper sauce

2 tablespoons packed brown sugar

Bread slices

---

1 Peel off plastic wrap of salami. Cut 12 crosswise (½-inch-deep) slits across top. Place, cut side up, in small dish that fits inside air fryer.

2 Combine preserves, hot pepper sauce and brown sugar in small bowl; stir well. Spoon sauce over top.

3 Preheat air fryer to 370°F. Cook 8 to 10 minutes or until juicy and dark brown, spooning sauce over salami occasionally during cooking.

4 Cut salami into thin slices; toss with sauce. Serve on bread.

EXTRAS: Serve with slices of challah bread or cocktail rye.

Must-Try Meals

PARMESAN-CRUSTED TILAPIA

makes 6 servings

⅔ cup plus 2 tablespoons grated
  Parmesan cheese, divided

⅔ cup panko bread crumbs

⅓ cup prepared light Alfredo sauce
  (refrigerated or jarred)

1½ teaspoons dried parsley flakes

6 tilapia fillets (4 ounces each)

Shaved Parmesan cheese
  (optional)

Minced fresh parsley (optional)

---

1 Combine ⅔ cup grated Parmesan cheese and panko in medium bowl; mix well. Combine Alfredo sauce, remaining 2 tablespoons grated cheese and parsley flakes in small bowl; mix well. Spread mixture over top of fish, coating in thick even layer. Top with panko mixture, pressing in gently to adhere.

2 Preheat air fryer to 390°F. Line basket with foil or parchment paper; spray with nonstick cooking spray.

3 Cook in batches 8 to 10 minutes or until crust is golden brown and fish begins to flake when tested with a fork. Garnish with shaved Parmesan cheese and fresh parsley.

BUTTERMILK AIR-FRIED CHICKEN

makes 4 servings

1 cut-up whole chicken (2½ to 3 pounds)

1 cup buttermilk

¾ cup all-purpose flour

½ teaspoon salt

½ teaspoon ground red pepper

¼ teaspoon garlic powder

2 cups plain dry bread crumbs

1 Place chicken pieces in large resealable food storage bag. Pour buttermilk over chicken. Close and refrigerate; let marinate at least 2 hours.

2 Combine flour, salt, red pepper and garlic powder in large shallow bowl. Place bread crumbs in another shallow bowl.

3 Preheat air fryer to 390°F. Spray basket with nonstick cooking spray.

4 Remove chicken pieces from buttermilk; coat with flour mixture then coat in bread crumbs. Spray chicken with cooking spray. Cook in batches 20 to 25 minutes or until brown and crisp on all sides and cooked through (165°F). Serve warm.

TERIYAKI SALMON

makes 2 servings

¼ cup dark sesame oil

Juice of 1 lemon

¼ cup soy sauce

2 tablespoons packed brown sugar

1 clove garlic, minced

2 salmon fillets (about 4 ounces each)

Hot cooked rice

Toasted sesame seeds and green onions (optional)

1 Whisk oil, lemon juice, soy sauce, brown sugar and garlic in medium bowl. Place salmon in large resealable food storage bag; add marinade. Refrigerate at least 2 hours.

2 Preheat air fryer to 350°F. Spray basket with nonstick cooking spray.

3 Cook 8 to 10 minutes or until salmon is crispy and easily flakes when tested with a fork. Serve with rice and garnish as desired.

VEGGIE PIZZA PITAS

makes 2 servings

1 whole wheat pita bread round, cut in half horizontally (to make 2 rounds)

2 tablespoons pizza sauce

1/2 teaspoon dried basil

1/8 teaspoon red pepper flakes (optional)

1/2 cup sliced mushrooms

1/4 cup thinly sliced green bell pepper

1/4 cup thinly sliced red onion

1/2 cup (4 ounces) shredded mozzarella cheese

1 teaspoon grated Parmesan cheese

1 Arrange pita rounds, rough sides up, in single layer on parchment paper. Spread 1 tablespoon pizza sauce evenly over each round to within 1/4 inch of edge. Sprinkle with basil and red pepper flakes, if desired. Top with mushrooms, bell pepper and onion. Sprinkle with mozzarella cheese.

2 Preheat air fryer to 370°F.

3 Cook in batches 5 to 7 minutes or until mozzarella cheese melts. Sprinkle 1/2 teaspoon Parmesan cheese over each pita round.

AIR-FRIED SALMON NUGGETS WITH BROCCOLI

makes 5 servings

1 pound skinless salmon fillet

2 eggs

1 cup plain dry bread crumbs

¾ teaspoon salt, divided

2 cups broccoli florets

1 tablespoon olive oil

Sweet and sour sauce or other favorite dipping sauce (optional)

1 Cut salmon into 1-inch chunks.

2 Whisk eggs in small bowl. Combine bread crumbs and ½ teaspoon salt in shallow dish. Dip salmon chunks in egg, letting excess drip back into dish. Coat evenly with bread crumbs. Set on plate; spray lightly with nonstick cooking spray.

3 Preheat air fryer to 390°F. Spray basket with cooking spray.

4 Cook in batches 3 to 4 minutes; flip nuggets over. Spray with cooking spray. Cook 3 to 4 minutes or until golden brown. Remove to plate; keep warm.

5 Meanwhile, toss broccoli with oil in large bowl. Sprinkle with remaining ¼ teaspoon salt. Cook 6 to 8 minutes or until browned and crispy.

6 Serve nuggets and broccoli with sweet and sour sauce or other dipping sauce, if desired.

SUBSTITUTE: Try garlic-herb or Italian-seasoned bread crumbs instead of plain.

EASY AIR-FRIED CHICKEN THIGHS

makes 4 servings

8 bone-in or boneless chicken thighs with skin (about 1½ pounds)
½ teaspoon garlic powder
½ teaspoon onion powder
½ teaspoon dried oregano
½ teaspoon ground thyme
½ teaspoon paprika
¼ teaspoon salt
½ teaspoon black pepper

1 Place chicken in large resealable food storage bag. Combine garlic powder, onion powder, oregano, thyme, paprika, salt and pepper in small bowl; mix well. Add to chicken; shake until spices are distributed.

2 Preheat air fryer to 350°F. Line basket with parchment paper; spray with nonstick cooking spray.

3 Cook in batches 20 to 25 minutes or until golden brown and cooked through (165°), turning chicken halfway through cooking.

STEAK, MUSHROOMS & ONIONS

makes 4 servings

3/4 pound boneless steak, cut into 1-inch cubes

8 ounces sliced mushrooms, cleaned and washed

1 small onion, chopped

3 tablespoons melted butter, divided

1 teaspoon Worcestershire sauce

1/2 teaspoon garlic powder

1/2 teaspoon salt

1/4 teaspoon black pepper

Hot cooked egg noodles (optional)

1/2 teaspoon dried parsley flakes

---

1 Combine steak pieces, mushrooms and onion in large bowl. Toss with 1 1/2 tablespoons butter, Worcestershire sauce and garlic powder.

2 Preheat air fryer to 390°F. Line basket with foil. Cook steak mixture 10 to 12 minutes, shaking occasionally, until steak is cooked.

3 Remove steak mixture to large bowl. Toss with remaining 1 1/2 tablespoons butter, salt and pepper.

4 Serve over noodles, if desired. Sprinkle with parsley flakes.

LEMON-PEPPER CHICKEN
makes 4 servings

⅓ cup lemon juice

¼ cup finely chopped onion

2 tablespoons olive oil

1 tablespoon packed brown sugar

1 tablespoon black pepper

3 cloves garlic, minced

2 teaspoons grated lemon peel

½ teaspoon salt

4 boneless skinless chicken breasts (about 1 pound)

---

1 Combine lemon juice, onion, oil, brown sugar, pepper, garlic, lemon peel and salt in small bowl; stir to blend. Pour marinade over chicken in large resealable food storage bag. Seal bag; knead to coat. Refrigerate at least 4 hours or overnight.

2 Preheat air fryer to 370°F. Line basket with parchment paper or foil; spray with nonstick cooking spray.

3 Remove chicken from marinade; discard marinade. Cook in batches 15 to 20 minutes or until chicken is browned and no longer pink in center.

ROAST DILL SCROD WITH ASPARAGUS

makes 4 servings

---

1 bunch (12 ounces) asparagus
   spears, ends trimmed

1 teaspoon olive oil

4 scrod or cod fillets (about
   5 ounces each)

1 tablespoon lemon juice

1 teaspoon dried dill weed

½ teaspoon salt

¼ teaspoon black pepper

   Paprika (optional)

---

1 Preheat air fryer to 390°F. Line basket with parchment paper.

2 Drizzle asparagus with oil. Roll asparagus to coat lightly with oil. Cook 8 to 10 minutes or until tender. Remove; keep warm.

3 Drizzle fish with lemon juice. Combine dill weed, salt and pepper in small bowl; sprinkle over fish.

4 Cook in batches 10 to 12 minutes or until fish is opaque in center and begins to flake when tested with a fork. Place fish and asparagus on serving plate. Sprinkle with paprika, if desired.

BANG-BANG CHICKEN ON RICE

makes 4 servings

CREAMY HOT SAUCE

- ½ cup mayonnaise
- ¼ cup sweet chili sauce
- 1½ teaspoons hot pepper sauce

CHICKEN

- 1 pound chicken breasts, cut into 1-inch pieces
- ¾ cup panko bread crumbs
- ½ cup all-purpose flour
- 2 green onions, chopped
- Hot cooked rice (optional)

1 Prepare Creamy Hot Sauce. Combine mayonnaise, chili sauce and hot pepper sauce in medium bowl. Divide mixture in half; set one half aside.

2 Put chicken in large bowl. Place panko in shallow dish.

3 Using hands, toss chicken with flour until well coated. Dip chicken pieces in Creamy Hot Sauce, then coat in panko. Spray with nonstick cooking spray.

4 Preheat air fryer to 390°F. Line basket with parchment paper.

5 Cook chicken in batches 10 to 12 minutes or until golden brown. Remove chicken to large bowl; drizzle with remaining Creamy Hot Sauce.

6 Sprinkle with green onions. Serve over rice, if desired.

FISH WITH LEMON TARRAGON "BUTTER"

makes 2 servings

---

2 teaspoons margarine

4 teaspoons lemon juice, divided

$\frac{1}{2}$ teaspoon grated lemon peel

$\frac{1}{4}$ teaspoon mustard

$\frac{1}{4}$ teaspoon dried tarragon

$\frac{1}{8}$ teaspoon salt

2 lean white fish fillets (4 ounces each),* rinsed and patted dry

$\frac{1}{4}$ teaspoon paprika

Cod, orange roughy, flounder, haddock, halibut and sole can be used.

---

1 Combine margarine, 2 teaspoons lemon juice, lemon peel, mustard, tarragon and salt in small bowl; mix well with a fork.

2 Preheat air fryer to 390°F. Spray basket with nonstick cooking spray. Drizzle fish with remaining 2 teaspoons lemon juice; sprinkle one side of each fillet with paprika.

3 Cook fish, paprika side down; 8 to 10 minutes until fish is opaque in center and begins to flake when tested with a fork. Top with margarine mixture.

CHILI PUFFS
makes 9 puffs

---

1 sheet frozen puff pastry (half of 17¼-ounce package), thawed

1 can (about 15 ounces) chili without beans

4 ounces cream cheese, softened

¼ cup (1 ounce) finely shredded sharp Cheddar cheese

Sliced green onions (optional)

---

1 Spray 2½-inch silicone muffin cups with nonstick cooking spray.

2 Roll out puff pastry on lightly floured surface. Cut nine (3-inch) squares.* Press dough into muffin cups.

3 Preheat air fryer to 390°F. Cook in batches 6 to 8 minutes or until golden brown. Cool slightly.

4 Meanwhile, combine chili and cream cheese in small saucepan over medium-low heat. Heat, stirring occasionally, until warmed and cream cheese blends into chili mixture. Remove from heat.

5 Fill each pastry shell with 2 teaspoons chili mixture, pressing down centers of pastry to fill, if necessary. Sprinkle evenly with Cheddar cheese. Garnish with green onions, if desired.

*Use a pizza cutter to easily cut puff pastry sheets.

SPICY SALMON
makes 4 servings

½ teaspoon ground cumin
½ teaspoon chili powder
¼ teaspoon salt

¼ teaspoon black pepper
¼ teaspoon paprika
4 salmon fillets (about 4 ounces each)

1 Combine cumin, chili powder, salt, pepper and paprika in small bowl. Rub over top of salmon.

2 Preheat air fryer to 350°F. Line basket with parchment paper; spray with nonstick cooking spray.

3 Cook in batches 8 to 10 minutes or until salmon is lightly crispy and easily flakes when tested with a fork.

SERVING SUGGESTION: Serve with tossed salad and rice.

PECAN-CRUSTED CHICKEN TENDERS

makes 4 servings

½ cup all-purpose flour	⅔ cup finely chopped pecans
½ cup milk	¾ teaspoon salt
1 egg	1¼ to 1½ pounds chicken tenders, cut in half lengthwise
1 cup cornflake cereal, crushed	

---

1 Place flour in shallow dish. Beat milk and egg in another shallow dish. Combine cornflake crumbs, chopped pecans and salt in third shallow dish. Dip both sides of chicken in flour, then in egg mixture, letting excess drip back into dish. Roll in crumb mixture to coat completely, pressing crumbs into chicken to adhere.

2 Preheat air fryer to 390°F. Line basket with foil; spray with nonstick cooking spray.

3 Cook in batches 18 to 20 minutes or until chicken is no longer pink in center. Cool completely.

BIG KID SHRIMP

makes 4 servings

½ cup plain dry bread crumbs

¼ cup grated Parmesan cheese

½ teaspoon paprika

½ teaspoon salt

⅛ teaspoon black pepper

2 tablespoons butter, melted

1 pound large raw shrimp, peeled and deveined (with tails on)

½ cup mayonnaise

½ cup ketchup

1 tablespoon sweet pickle relish

1 Combine bread crumbs, Parmesan cheese, paprika, salt and pepper in large bowl. Add butter; mix well. Rinse shrimp under cold water, drain. Toss with bread crumb mixture.

2 Preheat air fryer to 390°F. Line basket with parchment paper; spray with nonstick cooking spray.

3 Cook 5 to 7 minutes or until lightly browned and cooked through.

4 Combine mayonnaise, ketchup and relish in small bowl. Serve with shrimp.

MINI DIZZY DOGS >>

makes 4 to 5 servings

½ sheet refrigerated crescent roll dough (half of 8-ounce package)

20 mini hot dogs or smoked sausages

Ketchup and mustard

1 Cut dough lengthwise into 20 (¼-inch) strips. Coil 1 dough strip around 1 hot dog. Repeat with remaining dough strips and hot dogs.

2 Preheat air fryer to 370°F. Line basket with parchment paper.

3 Cook 5 to 6 minutes or until light golden brown. Serve with ketchup and mustard for dipping.

TUNA CAKES WITH CREAMY CUCUMBER SAUCE

makes 5 servings

½ cup finely chopped cucumber

6 ounces fat-free plain yogurt or fat-free plain Greek yogurt

1½ teaspoons chopped fresh dill *or* ½ teaspoon dried dill weed

1 teaspoon lemon-pepper seasoning

⅓ cup shredded carrots

¼ cup sliced green onions

¼ cup finely chopped celery

¼ cup mayonnaise

2 teaspoons spicy brown mustard

1 cup panko bread crumbs, divided

1 can (12 ounces) albacore tuna in water, drained

Lemon wedges (optional)

1 For sauce, stir together cucumber, yogurt, dill and lemon-pepper seasoning in small bowl. Cover and refrigerate until serving time.

2 In mixing bowl, combine carrots, green onions, celery, mayonnaise and mustard. Stir in ½ cup panko. Add tuna and mix until combined.

3 Place remaining ½ cup panko in shallow dish. Shape tuna mixture into five (½-inch-thick) patties. Dip patties in panko, lightly coating.

4 Preheat air fryer to 370°F. Spray basket with nonstick cooking spray.

5 Cook in batches 6 to 8 minutes, flipping halfway during cooking, until golden brown. Serve with yogurt mixture and garnish with lemon wedges.

COCONUT SHRIMP WITH PEAR CHUTNEY

makes 4 servings

Pear Chutney (recipe follows)

$\frac{1}{2}$ cup shredded unsweetened coconut

$\frac{3}{4}$ teaspoon curry powder

$\frac{1}{2}$ teaspoon salt

1 pound large raw shrimp, peeled and deveined (with tails on)

3 tablespoons melted unsalted butter

---

1. Prepare Pear Chutney; set aside. Combine coconut, curry powder and salt in shallow dish. Toss shrimp with melted butter to coat. Dip shrimp in coconut mixture, pressing lightly to adhere.

2. Preheat air fryer to 350°F. Spray air fryer basket with nonstick cooking spray.

3. Cook in batches 8 to 10 minutes, turning once halfway through cooking, until shrimp are pink and opaque. Serve with Pear Chutney.

PEAR CHUTNEY

makes 2 cups

---

1 tablespoon vegetable oil

1 jalapeño pepper,* seeded and minced

1 small shallot, minced

1 teaspoon grated fresh ginger

1 medium unpeeled ripe pear, cored and cut into $\frac{1}{2}$-inch pieces

2 teaspoons cider vinegar

1 teaspoon packed brown sugar

$\frac{1}{8}$ teaspoon salt

1 to 2 tablespoons water

1 tablespoon chopped green onion

Jalapeño peppers can sting and irritate the skin, so wear rubber gloves when handling peppers and do not touch your eyes.

---

1. Heat oil in medium saucepan over low heat. Add jalapeño pepper, shallot and ginger; cook and stir 3 minutes or until shallot is tender.

2. Add pear, vinegar, brown sugar and salt. Stir in 1 tablespoon water. Cover; cook over low heat 15 minutes or until pear is tender, adding additional 1 tablespoon water if mixture becomes dry. Stir in green onion; cook 1 minute. Let cool before serving.

Quick-Fix Sides

GARLIC ROASTED OLIVES AND TOMATOES >>

makes about 2 cups

1 cup assorted olives, pitted	1 tablespoon olive oil
1 cup grape tomatoes, halved	1 tablespoon herbes de Provence
4 cloves garlic, sliced	

1 Pat olives dry with paper towels.

2 Combine olives, tomatoes, garlic and oil in small bowl. Toss with herbes de Provence; mix well.

3 Preheat air fryer to 370°F. Cook 5 to 7 minutes or until browned and blistered, shaking occasionally during cooking. Remove to bowl.

SERVING SUGGESTION: Try tossing with hot cooked pasta for a main dish.

OLIVE TWISTS

makes 12 servings

1 package (8 ounces) refrigerated crescent roll dough	12 pimiento-stuffed green olives, chopped
1 egg white, beaten	½ teaspoon paprika

1 Roll dough on lightly floured work surface to 12×8-inch rectangle. Cut crescent dough into 12 strips.

2 Brush dough lightly with egg white; sprinkle with olives and paprika. Wrap dough around olive filling.

3 Preheat air fryer to 370°F. Line basket with parchment paper.

4 Cook 5 to 7 minutes or until golden brown.

ROASTED CHICKPEAS
makes 1 cup (about 4 servings)

1 can (about 15 ounces) chickpeas, rinsed and drained

1 tablespoon olive oil

¼ teaspoon salt

¼ teaspoon black pepper

¼ tablespoon chili powder

¼ teaspoon ground red pepper

1 lime, cut into wedges (optional)

1 Combine chickpeas, oil, salt and black pepper in large bowl; toss to mix well.

2 Preheat air fryer to 390°F.

3 Cook 8 to 10 minutes, shaking occasionally during cooking, until chickpeas begin to brown.

4 Sprinkle with chili powder and ground red pepper. Serve with lime wedges, if desired.

NOTE: Great as a snack or topping for salads. Chickpeas offer a delicious crunch and healthier alternative to croutons.

AIR-FRIED CORN-ON-THE-COB >>

makes 2 servings

2 teaspoons butter, melted
1/4 teaspoon salt
1/2 teaspoon black pepper
1/2 teaspoon chopped fresh parsley

2 ears corn, husks and silks removed
Foil
Grated Parmesan cheese (optional)

1. Combine butter, salt, pepper and parsley in small bowl. Brush corn with butter mixture. Wrap each ear of corn in foil.*

2. Preheat air fryer to 390°F. Cook 10 to 12 minutes, turning halfway through cooking. Sprinkle with Parmesan cheese before serving, if desired.

If your air fryer basket is on the smaller side, you may need to break ears of corn in half to fit.

KALE CHIPS

makes 6 servings

1 large bunch kale (about 1 pound)
1 tablespoon olive oil
1 teaspoon garlic powder

1/2 teaspoon salt
1/2 teaspoon black pepper

1. Wash kale and pat dry with paper towels. Remove center ribs and stems; discard. Cut leaves into 2- to 3-inch-wide pieces.

2. Combine kale leaves, oil, garlic powder, salt and pepper in large bowl; toss to coat.

3. Preheat air fryer to 390°F.

4. Cook in batches 3 to 4 minutes or until edges are lightly browned and leaves are crisp. Cool completely. Store in airtight container.

CHEESY GARLIC BREAD >>

makes 4 to 6 servings

---

1 loaf (about 8 ounces) Italian bread

¼ cup (½ stick) butter, softened

4 cloves garlic, diced

2 tablespoons grated Parmesan cheese

1 cup (4 ounces) shredded mozzarella cheese

---

1 Cut bread in half horizontally. Spread cut sides of bread evenly with butter; top with garlic. Sprinkle with Parmesan, then mozzarella cheeses.

2 Preheat air fryer to 370°F. Line basket with foil.

3 Cook 5 to 6 minutes or until cheese is melted and golden brown. Cut crosswise into slices. Serve warm.

EGGPLANT NIBBLES

makes 4 servings

---

1 egg

1 tablespoon water

½ cup seasoned dry bread crumbs

1 Asian eggplant or 1 small globe eggplant

Marinara sauce (optional)

---

1 Beat egg and water in shallow dish. Place bread crumbs in another shallow dish.

2 Cut ends off of eggplant. Cut into sticks about 3 inches long by ½-inch wide.

3 Coat eggplant sticks in egg, letting excess drip back into dish, then roll in bread crumbs. Spray with olive oil cooking spray.

4 Preheat air fryer to 370°F. Line basket with foil or parchment paper.

5 Cook in batches 12 to 14 minutes, shaking occasionally during cooking, until eggplant is tender and lightly browned. Serve with marinara sauce, if desired.

AIR-FRIED CAULIFLOWER FLORETS >>

makes 4 servings

1 head cauliflower	2 tablespoons panko bread crumbs
1 tablespoon olive oil	1/2 teaspoon salt
3 tablespoons grated Parmesan cheese	1/2 teaspoon chopped fresh parsley
	1/4 teaspoon ground black pepper

1 Cut cauliflower into florets. Place in large bowl. Drizzle with oil. Sprinkle Parmesan cheese, panko, salt, parsley and pepper over cauliflower; toss to coat.

2 Preheat air fryer to 390°F. Spray basket with nonstick cooking spray.

3 Cook in batches 18 to 20 minutes or until browned, shaking every 6 minutes during cooking.

ROASTED ASPARAGUS

makes 4 servings

1 bunch (14 ounces) asparagus spears	1/4 teaspoon black pepper
1 tablespoon olive oil	1/4 cup shredded Asiago or Parmesan cheese (optional)
1/2 teaspoon salt	

1 Trim off and discard tough ends of asparagus spears. Peel stem ends with vegetable peeler, if desired. Arrange asparagus in shallow baking dish; drizzle with oil, rolling spears to coat. Sprinkle with salt and pepper.

2 Preheat air fryer to 390°F.

3 Cook in batches 8 to 10 minutes, shaking occasionally during cooking, until tender. Sprinkle with cheese, if desired.

PEPPERONI BREAD

makes about 6 servings

1 package (about 14 ounces) refrigerated pizza dough

8 slices provolone cheese

20 to 30 slices pepperoni (about 1/2 of 6-ounce package)

3/4 cup (3 ounces) shredded mozzarella cheese

1/2 cup grated Parmesan cheese

1/2 teaspoon Italian seasoning

1 egg, beaten

Marinara sauce, heated

1 Unroll pizza dough on lightly floured surface; cut dough in half.

2 Working with one half at a time, arrange half the provolone slices on half the dough. Top with half the pepperoni, half the mozzarella and Parmesan cheeses and half the Italian seasoning. Repeat with other half dough and toppings.

3 Fold top half of dough over filling; press edges with fork or pinch edges to seal.

4 Preheat air fryer to 390°F. Line basket with parchment paper. Transfer one bread to basket. Brush with egg.

5 Cook 8 to 10 minutes or until crust is golden brown. Remove to wire rack to cool slightly. Repeat with other bread. Cut crosswise into slices; serve warm with marinara sauce.

ZUCCHINI FRITTE

makes 4 servings

Lemon Aioli (recipe follows)

¾ to 1 cup soda water

½ cup all-purpose flour

¼ cup cornstarch

½ teaspoon coarse salt, plus additional for serving

¼ teaspoon garlic powder

¼ teaspoon dried oregano

¼ teaspoon black pepper

3 cups panko bread crumbs

1½ pounds medium zucchini (about 8 inches long), ends trimmed, cut lengthwise into ¼-inch-thick slices

¼ cup grated Parmesan or Romano cheese

Chopped fresh parsley

Lemon wedges

1 Prepare Lemon Aioli; cover and refrigerate until ready to use.

2 Pour ¾ cup soda water into large bowl. Combine flour, cornstarch, ½ teaspoon salt, garlic powder, oregano and pepper in medium bowl; mix well. Gradually whisk flour mixture into soda water just until blended. Add additional soda water, if necessary, to reach consistency of thin pancake batter. Place panko in shallow dish.

3 Working with one at a time, dip zucchini slices into batter to coat; let excess batter drip back into bowl. Add to panko; pressing into zucchini slices to coat both sides completely.

4 Preheat air fryer to 390°F. Line basket with parchment paper.

5 Cook in batches 7 to 10 minutes or until golden brown. Sprinkle with cheese and parsley. Serve with Lemon Aioli and lemon wedges.

LEMON AIOLI: Combine ½ cup mayonnaise, 2 tablespoons lemon juice, 1 tablespoon chopped fresh Italian parsley and 1 clove minced garlic in small bowl; mix well. Season with salt and pepper.

ORANGE GLAZED CARROTS

makes 6 servings

---

1 package (32 ounces) baby carrots

1 tablespoon packed light brown sugar

1 tablespoon orange juice

1 tablespoon melted butter

$\frac{1}{4}$ teaspoon ground cinnamon

$\frac{1}{8}$ teaspoon ground nutmeg

Orange peel and fresh chopped parsley (optional)

---

1 Place carrots in large bowl. Combine brown sugar, orange juice and butter in small bowl. Pour over carrots; toss well.

2 Preheat air fryer to 390°F.

3 Cook 6 to 8 minutes, shaking occasionally during cooking, until carrots are tender and lightly browned. Remove to serving dish. Sprinkle with cinnamon and nutmeg. Garnish with orange peel and parsley.

CURLY AIR-FRIED FRIES

makes 4 servings

---

2 large russet potatoes, unpeeled

¼ cup finely chopped onion

1 teaspoon vegetable oil

½ teaspoon salt

¼ teaspoon black pepper

Honey mustard dipping sauce, ketchup or other favorite dipping sauce

---

1 Spiral potatoes with thick spiral blade of spiralizer.*

2 Place potatoes and onion in large bowl; drizzle with oil. Toss well.

3 Preheat air fryer to 390°F. Line basket with parchment paper. Cook 12 to 15 minutes or until golden brown and crispy, shaking occasionally during cooking. Sprinkle with salt and pepper.

4 Serve with dipping sauce.

*If you do not have a spiralizer, cut potatoes into thin strips.

FRIED GREEN TOMATO PARMESAN

makes 2 servings

---

1 can (15 ounces) no-salt-added
    tomato sauce, divided
2 green tomatoes
    Salt and black pepper
1/4 cup all-purpose flour
1/2 teaspoon Italian seasoning

1 egg
1 tablespoon water
3/4 cup panko bread crumbs
1/4 cup shredded Parmesan cheese
    Shredded fresh basil
    Hot cooked spaghetti (optional)

---

1   Spread 1/2 cup tomato sauce in small baking dish that fits inside air fryer basket.

2   Cut tomatoes into 1/4-inch slices. Lightly season with salt and pepper, if desired.

3   Combine flour and Italian seasoning in shallow dish. Whisk egg and water in another shallow dish. Place panko in third shallow dish. Coat tomatoes with flour mixture. Dip in egg mixture. Dredge in panko, pressing onto all sides.

4   Preheat air fryer to 350°F. Line basket with parchment paper. Cook tomatoes in batches 2 to 3 minutes per side or until panko is golden brown. Remove tomatoes to sauce in baking dish, slightly overlapping. Sprinkle with Parmesan cheese and 1/2 cup tomato sauce.

5   Cook 6 to 8 minutes or until cheese is melted and sauce is heated through. Sprinkle with basil. Serve with spaghetti, if desired, and remaining tomato sauce.

POTATO BALLS

makes 20 balls

---

2 cups refrigerated leftover mashed potatoes*

2 tablespoons all-purpose flour, plus additional for rolling balls

2/3 cup shredded reduced-fat Cheddar cheese

1/4 cup chopped green onions

1 large egg

1/2 teaspoon salt

1/4 teaspoon black pepper

1 1/2 cups seasoned dry bread crumbs

If you don't have leftover potatoes, prepare 2 cups instant mashed potatoes and refrigerate at least 1 hour.

---

1 Combine potatoes, 2 tablespoons flour, cheese and green onions in large bowl. Scoop out about 2 tablespoons mixture and roll into a 1-inch ball, adding additional flour, if necessary, making about 20 balls.

2 Beat egg, salt and pepper in medium bowl. Place bread crumbs in shallow dish. Dip balls in egg, letting excess drip back into bowl, then roll in bread crumbs until fully coated. Place on baking sheet; refrigerate 30 minutes.

3 Preheat air fryer to 390°F. Spray basket with nonstick cooking spray.

4 Cook in batches 8 to 10 minutes or until balls are browned and heated through.

ZUCCHINI TOMATO ROUNDS

makes 4 servings

---

2 large zucchini

Foil

½ cup cherry tomatoes, sliced

1 tablespoon olive oil

2 cloves garlic, minced

2 teaspoons Italian seasoning

1 teaspoon grated Parmesan cheese

---

1 Cut zucchini into thin slices three-fourths of the way down (do not cut all the way through). Place zucchini on foil sprayed with nonstick cooking spray.

2 Place tomato slices between each zucchini slice. Combine oil and garlic in small bowl. Drizzle over zucchini. Sprinkle with Italian seasoning and Parmesan cheese. Wrap foil around zucchini.

3 Preheat air fryer to 390°F. Place foil packets in basket. Cook 10 to 12 minutes or until browned and softened.

GARLIC AIR-FRIED FRIES

makes 4 servings

2 large potatoes, peeled and cut into matchstick strips

2 teaspoons plus 1 tablespoon olive oil, divided

1½ teaspoons minced garlic

½ teaspoon dried parsley flakes

½ teaspoon salt

¼ teaspoon ground black pepper

Ketchup, blue cheese or ranch dressing (optional)

1 Preheat air fryer to 390°F. Line basket with parchment paper.

2 Combine potato strips and 2 teaspoons oil in medium bowl; toss well.

3 Cook in batches 8 to 10 minutes, tossing occasionally, until golden brown and crispy.

4 While fries are cooking, combine remaining 1 tablespoon oil, garlic, parsley flakes, salt and pepper in small bowl.

5 Toss warm fries with garlic sauce. Serve immediately with ketchup, blue cheese or ranch dressing.

CORNMEAL-CRUSTED CAULIFLOWER STEAKS

makes 4 servings

½ cup cornmeal

¼ cup all-purpose flour

1 teaspoon salt

1 teaspoon dried sage

½ teaspoon garlic powder

¼ teaspoon black pepper

½ cup milk

2 heads cauliflower

2 tablespoons butter, melted

Barbecue sauce (optional)

1 Combine cornmeal, flour, salt, sage, garlic powder and pepper in shallow dish. Pour milk into another shallow dish.

2 Turn cauliflower stem side up on cutting board. Trim away leaves, leaving stem intact. Slice through stem into 2 or 3 slices. Trim off excess florets from two end slices, creating flat "steaks." Repeat with remaining cauliflower; reserve extra cauliflower for another use.

3 Dip cauliflower into milk to coat both sides. Place in cornmeal mixture; pat onto all sides of cauliflower. Drizzle butter evenly over cauliflower.

4 Preheat air fryer to 390°F. Line basket with parchment paper.

5 Cook in batches 12 to 15 minutes, flipping halfway through cooking, until cauliflower is tender. Serve with barbecue sauce for dipping, if desired.

THICK POTATO CHIPS WITH BEER KETCHUP

makes 4 servings

Beer Ketchup (recipe follows)	Sea salt and black pepper
2 baking potatoes, unpeeled	

1 Prepare Beer Ketchup; set aside.

2 Slice potatoes into $\frac{1}{8}$- to $\frac{1}{4}$-inch-thick slices; place in large bowl. Spray with nonstick cooking spray. Sprinkle with salt and pepper.

3 Preheat air fryer to 390°F. Cook in batches 12 to 15 minutes, shaking occasionally during cooking, until crispy and golden brown.

4 Serve potatoes with Beer Ketchup.

BEER KETCHUP

makes about 1 cup

$\frac{3}{4}$ cup ketchup	$\frac{1}{4}$ teaspoon onion powder
$\frac{1}{4}$ cup beer	Ground red pepper
1 tablespoon Worcestershire sauce	

Mix all ingredients in small saucepan. Bring to a boil. Reduce heat; simmer 2 to 3 minutes. Remove from heat and let cool. Cover and store in refrigerator until ready to use.

SPEEDY SALAMI SPIRALS
makes about 28 spirals

1 package (about 14 ounces) refrigerated pizza dough

1 cup (4 ounces) shredded Italian cheese blend

3 to 4 ounces thinly sliced Genoa salami

1 Unroll dough on cutting board or clean work surface; press into 15×10-inch rectangle. Sprinkle evenly with cheese; top with salami.

2 Starting with long side, tightly roll up dough and filling jelly-roll style, pinching seam to seal. Cut roll crosswise into 1/2-inch slices. (If roll is too soft to cut, refrigerate or freeze until firm.)

3 Preheat air fryer to 390°F. Line basket with parchment paper.

4 Cook in batches 8 to 10 minutes or until golden brown. Serve warm.

BACON-ROASTED BRUSSELS SPROUTS >>

makes 4 servings

---

1 pound Brussels sprouts

2 slices bacon, cut into ½-inch pieces

2 teaspoons packed brown sugar

Salt and black pepper

---

1 Trim ends from Brussels sprouts; cut in half lengthwise.

2 Combine Brussels sprouts, bacon and brown sugar in large bowl.

3 Preheat air fryer to 390°F. Cook 15 to 18 minutes, shaking occasionally during cooking, until golden brown. Season with salt and pepper.

SAVORY STUFFED TOMATOES

makes 4 servings

---

2 large ripe tomatoes (1 to 1¼ pounds total)

¾ cup garlic- or Caesar-flavored croutons

¼ cup chopped pitted kalamata olives (optional)

2 tablespoons chopped fresh basil

1 clove garlic, minced

2 tablespoons grated Parmesan or Romano cheese

1 tablespoon olive oil

---

1 Cut tomatoes in half crosswise; discard seeds. Scrape out and reserve pulp. Set aside tomato shells.

2 Chop up tomato pulp; place in medium bowl. Add croutons, olives, if desired, basil and garlic; toss well. Spoon mixture into tomato shells. Sprinkle with Parmesan cheese; drizzle oil over shells.

3 Preheat air fryer to 350°F. Line basket with foil or parchment paper.

4 Cook 5 to 7 minutes or until heated through.

ORANGE AND MAPLE-GLAZED ROASTED BEETS
makes 4 servings

4 medium beets, scrubbed

¼ cup orange juice

3 tablespoons balsamic or cider vinegar

2 tablespoons maple syrup

2 teaspoons grated orange peel, divided

1 teaspoon Dijon mustard

Salt and black pepper

1 to 2 tablespoons chopped fresh mint (optional)

1 Peel and cut beets in half lengthwise; cut into wedges. Place in large bowl.

2 Whisk orange juice, vinegar, maple syrup, 1 teaspoon orange peel and mustard in small bowl until well blended. Pour half over beets.

3 Preheat air fryer to 390°F.

4 Cook 22 to 25 minutes, shaking occasionally during cooking, until softened. Remove to serving dish; pour remaining orange juice mixture over beets. Season with salt and pepper. Sprinkle with remaining 1 teaspoon orange peel and mint, if desired.

SERVING SUGGESTION: The flavors of this recipe make it a great side dish to serve at your holiday meal.

SWEET POTATO FRIES >>

makes 2 servings

---

2 sweet potatoes, peeled and sliced
1 tablespoon olive oil

¼ teaspoon coarse salt
¼ teaspoon black pepper

---

1 Toss potatoes with oil, salt and pepper in medium bowl.

2 Preheat air fryer to 390°F. Spray basket with nonstick cooking spray.

3 Cook 10 to 12 minutes, shaking occasionally during cooking, until lightly browned.

CRISPY FRIES WITH HERBED DIPPING SAUCE

makes 3 servings

Herbed Dipping Sauce (recipe follows)
2 large unpeeled baking potatoes

1 tablespoon vegetable oil
½ teaspoon kosher salt

---

1 Prepare Herbed Dipping Sauce; set aside.

2 Cut potatoes into ¼-inch strips. Toss potato strips with oil in large bowl to coat evenly.

3 Preheat air fryer to 390°F. Spray basket with nonstick cooking spray.

4 Cook in batches 18 to 20 minutes, shaking occasionally during cooking, until golden brown and crispy. Sprinkle with salt. Serve immediately with Herbed Dipping Sauce.

HERBED DIPPING SAUCE: Stir ¼ cup mayonnaise, 1 tablespoon chopped fresh herbs (such as basil, parsley, oregano and/or dill), ¼ teaspoon salt and ⅛ teaspoon black pepper in small bowl until smooth and well blended. Cover and refrigerate until ready to serve.

PESTO-PARMESAN TWISTS

makes 24 breadsticks

---

1 package (about 11 ounces) refrigerated bread dough

1/4 cup prepared pesto

2/3 cup grated Parmesan cheese, divided

1 tablespoon olive oil

---

1 Roll out dough into 20×10-inch rectangle on lightly floured surface. Spread pesto evenly over half of dough; sprinkle with 1/3 cup Parmesan cheese. Fold remaining half of dough over filling, forming 10-inch square.

2 Cut into 12 (1-inch) strips with sharp knife. Cut strips in half crosswise to form 24 strips total. Twist each strip several times.

3 Brush breadsticks with oil; sprinkle with remaining 1/3 cup Parmesan cheese.

4 Preheat air fryer to 370°F. Cook in batches 8 to 10 minutes or until golden brown. Serve warm.

Guilty Pleasures

TOASTED POUND CAKE WITH BERRIES AND CREAM >>

makes 4 servings

---

1 frozen pound cake, thawed

2 tablespoons melted butter

1 cup fresh blackberries or blueberries

1 cup fresh raspberries or strawberries

Whipped topping, vanilla ice cream or prepared lemon curd

---

1 Cut pound cake into eight slices. Brush both sides of cake with butter.

2 Preheat air fryer to 370°F. Cook in batches 5 to 7 minutes, turning halfway through cooking, until cake is lightly browned.

3 Serve with fresh berries, whipped topping, ice cream or lemon curd, as desired.

PEACHES WITH RASPBERRY SAUCE

makes 4 servings

---

1 package (10 ounces) frozen raspberries, thawed

1½ teaspoons lemon juice

2 tablespoons packed brown sugar

½ teaspoon ground cinnamon

1 can (15 ounces) peach halves in juice (4 halves)

Foil

2 teaspoons butter, cut into small pieces

Fresh mint sprigs (optional)

---

1 Combine raspberries and lemon juice in food processor fitted with metal blade; process until smooth. Refrigerate until ready to serve.

2 Preheat air fryer to 350°F.

3 Combine brown sugar and cinnamon in medium bowl; coat peach halves with mixture. Place peach halves, cut sides up, on foil. Dot with butter. Fold foil over peaches. Place packet in basket.

4 Cook 6 to 8 minutes or until peaches are soft and lightly browned.

5 To serve, spoon 2 tablespoons raspberry sauce over each peach half. Garnish with mint.

DOUGHNUT HOLE FONDUE

makes 5 servings

---

1 package (about 6 ounces) refrigerated biscuit dough (5 biscuits)

3 tablespoons butter, divided

1 tablespoon sugar

1/4 teaspoon ground cinnamon

3/4 cup whipping cream

1 cup bittersweet or semisweet chocolate chips

1/2 teaspoon vanilla

Sliced fresh fruit, such as pineapple, strawberries and cantaloupe

---

1 Separate biscuits into five portions. Cut each in half; roll dough into balls to create 10 balls.

2 Place 2 tablespoons butter in small microwavable bowl. Microwave on HIGH 30 seconds or until melted; stir. Combine sugar and cinnamon in small dish. Dip balls in melted butter; roll in cinnamon-sugar mixture.

3 Preheat air fryer to 370°F. Spray basket with nonstick cooking spray.

4 Cook in batches 4 to 5 minutes or until golden brown.

5 Meanwhile, heat cream in small saucepan until bubbles form around edge. Remove from heat. Add chocolate; let stand 2 minutes or until softened. Add remaining 1 tablespoon butter and vanilla; whisk until smooth. Keep warm in fondue pot or transfer to serving bowl.

6 Serve with doughnut holes and fruit.

CHOCOLATE-COFFEE NAPOLEONS

makes 6 napoleons

---

1 tablespoon instant coffee
   granules

¼ cup warm water

1 package (4-serving size)
   chocolate instant pudding and
   pie filling mix

1¾ cups whole milk plus 1 teaspoon
   whole milk, divided

1 sheet frozen puff pastry (half of a
   17¼-ounce package), thawed

3 tablespoons powdered sugar

2 tablespoons bittersweet or
   semisweet chocolate chips

---

1 Dissolve coffee in water in small bowl; set aside to cool.

2 Combine pudding mix, 1¾ cups milk and coffee in medium bowl; mix according to package directions. Cover and refrigerate until needed.

3 Preheat air fryer to 370°F. Unfold pastry sheet; cut into three strips along fold marks. Cut each strip crosswise into thirds, forming nine squares total. Cook in batches 8 to 10 minutes or until puffed and golden brown. Remove to wire rack to cool completely.

4 Blend powdered sugar and remaining 1 teaspoon milk in small bowl until smooth. Cut each pastry square in half crosswise with serrated knife to form 18 pieces total. Spread powdered sugar icing over tops of six pastry pieces.

5 Place chocolate chips in small resealable food storage bag. Microwave on MEDIUM (50%) 30 seconds or until melted. Cut small piece off one corner of bag; drizzle over iced pastry pieces. Place in refrigerator while assembling napoleons.

6 Spoon about 2 tablespoons pudding mixture over each of six pastry pieces; layer with remaining six pastry pieces and pudding mixture. Top with iced pastry pieces. Refrigerate until ready to serve.

MIXED BERRY DESSERT LAVASH WITH HONEYED MASCARPONE

makes 4 servings

1½ cups assorted mixed fresh berries

2 tablespoons honey, divided

½ teaspoon vanilla

1 piece lavash bread, 7½×9½ inches

1 tablespoon melted butter

4 ounces (½ cup) mascarpone cheese

1 tablespoon julienned fresh mint leaves

1 Place berries in medium bowl; stir in 1 tablespoon honey and vanilla. Refrigerate until ready to use.

2 Brush both sides of lavash with butter; cut into four even pieces.

3 Preheat air fryer to 370°F. Line basket with parchment paper. Cook 6 to 8 minutes, turning half way through cooking, until lavash is golden and crisp. Cool 5 minutes on wire rack.

4 Stir mascarpone and remaining 1 tablespoon honey in small bowl. Spread over each piece of lavash. Top with sweetened berries. Sprinkle with mint to serve.

UPSIDE-DOWN APPLES

makes 2 servings

Foil

2 tablespoons finely chopped pecans or walnuts

2 tablespoons chopped dried apricots or any dried fruit

1/4 teaspoon ground cinnamon

1/4 teaspoon vanilla

1/8 teaspoon ground nutmeg

1/8 teaspoon salt

1 tablespoon honey or maple syrup

1 Fuji apple (about 8 ounces), halved and cored

1/2 cup vanilla ice cream (optional)

1 Cut two 12×12-inch pieces foil; spray with nonstick cooking spray.

2 Combine pecans, apricots, cinnamon, vanilla, nutmeg and salt in small bowl; mix well. Spread over foil. Drizzle with honey. Place apple halves on top of nut mixture, cut side down. Wrap foil around apple.

3 Preheat air fryer to 370°F. Cook 20 to 22 minutes or just until tender. Serve apple and nut mixture with ice cream, if desired.

TIP: Fuji apples are a combination of Red Delicious and Ralls Janet apples. They are crisp and juicy apples that hold their shape when baking. If Fuji apples are not available, substitute Braeburn or Gala apples.

CHOCOLATE-COVERED BACON

makes 12 slices

12 slices bacon	2 tablespoons shortening, divided
12 wooden skewers (12 inches)	1 cup white chocolate chips or butterscotch chips
1 cup semisweet chocolate chips	

1 Preheat air fryer to 390°F. Thread each bacon slice onto wooden skewer.*

2 Cook 6 to 8 minutes or until crispy. Remove to paper-towel lined plate. Cool completely.

3 Combine semisweet chocolate chips and 1 tablespoon shortening in large microwavable bowl. Microwave on HIGH at 30-second intervals until melted and smooth.

4 Combine white chocolate chips or butterscotch chips and remaining 1 tablespoon shortening in large microwavable bowl. Microwave on HIGH at 30-second intervals until melted and smooth.

5 Drizzle chocolates over each bacon slice as desired. Place on parchment paper-lined baking sheets. Refrigerate until firm. Store in refrigerator.

Soak skewers in cold water 20 minutes to prevent burning.

HASSELBACK APPLES

makes 4 servings

---

2 medium apples, unpeeled
    Foil
2 tablespoons packed brown sugar
2 tablespoons finely chopped
    walnuts

$\frac{1}{2}$ teaspoon ground cinnamon
2 tablespoons butter, melted
$\frac{1}{2}$ cup vanilla ice cream (optional)

---

1 Cut apples in half vertically. Scoop out seeds. Lay flat side down; cut slits $\frac{1}{8}$ inch apart almost all the way down. Place apples on foil; wrapping lightly up sides of apple.

2 Combine brown sugar, walnuts and cinnamon in small bowl. Brush butter over tops of apples, letting drip inside slits. Sprinkle apples with brown sugar mixture.

3 Preheat air fryer to 350°F. Place foil-wrapped apples in basket. Cook 12 to 15 minutes or until apples are softened and browned.

4 Serve with ice cream, if desired.

NOTE: If apples brown too quickly on top, brush with additional melted butter.

TROPICAL PINEAPPLE RINGS

makes 10 servings

---

1 can (20 ounces) pineapple slices
   in pineapple juice

1 teaspoon coconut extract

2 eggs

½ cup all-purpose flour

1 cup unsweetened shredded
   coconut

1 cup panko bread crumbs

Powdered sugar, maraschino
   cherries (optional)

---

1 Drain pineapple slices, reserving juice. Place pineapple in large resealable food storage bag; add ¼ cup reserved pineapple juice and coconut extract. Refrigerate at least 15 minutes.

2 Whisk eggs and remaining ½ cup pineapple juice in medium bowl.

3 Place flour in shallow dish. Combine coconut and panko in another shallow dish.

4 Remove pineapple from refrigerator; drain juice. Pat slices dry with paper towels.

5 Coat pineapple with flour. Dip in egg mixture, letting excess drip back into bowl, then coat with coconut-panko mixture. Set pineapple on baking sheet. Refrigerate 15 minutes.

6 Preheat air fryer to 350°F. Spray basket with nonstick cooking spray.

7 Cook in batches 5 to 6 minutes or until coating is lightly browned and toasted. Serve warm. Sprinkle with powdered sugar and cherries, if desired.

APPLE PIE POCKETS

makes 4 servings

2 pieces lavash bread, each cut into
    4 rectangles
2 tablespoons melted butter
¾ cup apple pie filling
1 egg, lightly beaten with
    1 teaspoon water

½ cup powdered sugar
⅛ teaspoon ground cinnamon
2½ teaspoons milk

1 Brush one side of each piece of lavash with butter. Place half of the pieces, buttered-side down, on work surface. Spoon 3 tablespoons pie filling in center of each lavash, leaving ½-inch border uncovered. Using pastry brush, brush border with egg wash. Top with remaining lavash pieces, buttered-side up. Using tines of fork, press edges together to seal. Use paring knife to cut 3 small slits in center of each pie pocket.

2 Preheat air fryer to 370°F. Line basket with parchment paper.

3 Cook in batches 8 to 10 minutes or until crust is golden and crisp. Remove to wire rack; cool 15 minutes.

4 Combine powdered sugar, cinnamon and milk in small bowl; whisk until smooth. Drizzle over pockets; let stand 15 minutes to allow glaze to slightly set.

RASPBERRY WHITE CHOCOLATE DANISH >>

makes 8 servings

1 package (8 ounces) refrigerated
   crescent roll dough
8 teaspoons red raspberry
   preserves

1 ounce white baking chocolate,
   chopped

1 Unroll crescent dough; separate into eight triangles. Place 1 teaspoon preserves in center of each triangle. Fold right and left corners of long side over filling to top corner to form rectangle. Pinch edges to seal.

2 Preheat air fryer to 370°F. Line basket with parchment paper; spray with nonstick cooking spray.

3 Cook in batches, seam side up, 5 to 7 minutes or until lightly browned. Remove to wire rack to cool 5 minutes.

4 Place white chocolate in small resealable food storage bag. Microwave on MEDIUM (50%) 1 minute; gently knead bag. Microwave and knead at additional 30-second intervals until chocolate is completely melted. Cut off small corner of bag; drizzle chocolate over danish.

POUND CAKE DIP STICKS

makes 8 to 10 servings

1/2 cup raspberry jam, divided
1 package (10 3/4 ounces) frozen
   pound cake

1 1/2 cups cold whipping cream

1 Microwave 1/4 cup jam on HIGH 30 seconds or until smooth. Cut pound cake into 10 (1/2-inch) slices. Brush one side of slices lightly with warm jam. Cut each slice lengthwise into three sticks.

2 Preheat air fryer to 390°F. Spray basket with nonstick cooking spray.

3 Cook in batches 5 to 6 minutes or until cake sticks are crisp and light golden brown. Remove to wire rack.

4 Meanwhile, beat whipping cream in large bowl with electric mixer until soft peaks form. Add remaining 1/4 cup raspberry jam; beat until combined. Serve pound cake dip sticks with raspberry whipped cream.

PINEAPPLE WITH SPICED VANILLA SAUCE

makes 2 servings

3 ounces cream cheese

¼ cup granulated sugar

¼ cup half-and-half

¼ teaspoon pumpkin pie spice

¼ teaspoon vanilla

1 sheet (14×12 inches) heavy-duty foil

2 teaspoons butter

2 thick round slices fresh pineapple, skin and eyes trimmed

1 tablespoon light brown sugar

1 Place cream cheese, granulated sugar, half-and-half, pumpkin pie spice and vanilla in food processor or blender; process until smooth. Refrigerate.

2 Coat center of foil sheet with butter. Place pineapple slices side by side on foil. Sprinkle with brown sugar. Fold up sides and ends of foil around pineapple, leaving top open.

3 Preheat air fryer to 350°F. Cook 10 to 12 minutes or until surface of pineapple is bubbling and browned.

4 Transfer pineapple to serving plates. Serve immediately with cream cheese mixture.

CANDY CALZONE >>

makes 16 servings

1 package small chocolate, peanut and nougat candy bars, chocolate peanut butter cups or other chocolate candy bar (8 bars)	1 package (about 15 ounces) refrigerated pie crusts (2 crusts)
	½ cup milk chocolate chips

1 Chop candy into ¼-inch pieces.

2 Unroll pie crusts on cutting board or clean surface. Cut out 3-inch circles with biscuit cutter. Place about 1 tablespoon chopped candy on one side of each circle; fold dough over candy to form semicircle. Crimp edges with fingers or fork to seal.

3 Preheat air fryer to 370°F. Line basket with parchment paper. Cook in batches 8 to 10 minutes or until golden brown. Remove to wire rack to cool slightly.

4 Place chocolate chips in small microwavable bowl; microwave on HIGH 1 minute. Stir; microwave in 30-second intervals, stirring until smooth. Drizzle melted chocolate over calzones; serve warm.

BAKED PEARS

makes 4 servings

1 tablespoon sugar	2 teaspoons butter
¼ teaspoon ground cinnamon	½ cup pear juice, divided
2 medium ripe Bosc pears, halved lengthwise and cored	3 gingersnap cookies, crushed

1 Combine sugar and cinnamon in small bowl; sprinkle over pear halves. Place ½ teaspoon butter in each pear cavity. Drizzle 1 tablespoon juice over top of each pear.

2 Preheat air fryer to 370°F. Spray basket with nonstick cooking spray. Place pear halves, cut sides up, in basket.

3 Cook 12 to 14 minutes or until pears are browned. Sprinkle with crushed gingersnaps; cook 3 to 4 minutes. Drizzle remaining ¼ cup juice over pears to serve.

CHOCOLATE-PEANUT BUTTER BANANAS

makes 2 servings

¼ cup chocolate syrup	1 tablespoon packed brown sugar
1 tablespoon peanut butter	1 cup vanilla ice cream
1 large firm banana, unpeeled	2 tablespoons chopped peanuts
1 teaspoon melted butter	

1 Place chocolate syrup in small microwavable bowl; microwave on HIGH 10 to 15 seconds or until warm. Slowly whisk in peanut butter until well blended. Keep warm until ready to serve.

2 Preheat air fryer to 350°F. Line basket with foil or parchment paper. Cut unpeeled banana in half lengthwise. Brush cut sides with butter; place cut side down in basket. Cook 1½ to 2 minutes. Turn banana; spread brown sugar over banana. Cook 1 to 2 minutes or until brown sugar melts and banana softens.

3 Peel banana; cut each piece in half. Place two pieces in each serving dish. Top with ice cream. Drizzle with warm chocolate sauce; sprinkle with peanuts.

NOTE: To chop peanuts, place in small resealable food storage bag and crush slightly with a meat mallet.

METRIC CONVERSION CHART

VOLUME MEASUREMENTS (dry)

1/8 teaspoon = 0.5 mL
1/4 teaspoon = 1 mL
1/2 teaspoon = 2 mL
3/4 teaspoon = 4 mL
1 teaspoon = 5 mL
1 tablespoon = 15 mL
2 tablespoons = 30 mL
1/4 cup = 60 mL
1/3 cup = 75 mL
1/2 cup = 125 mL
2/3 cup = 150 mL
3/4 cup = 175 mL
1 cup = 250 mL
2 cups = 1 pint = 500 mL
3 cups = 750 mL
4 cups = 1 quart = 1 L

VOLUME MEASUREMENTS (fluid)

1 fluid ounce (2 tablespoons) = 30 mL
4 fluid ounces (1/2 cup) = 125 mL
8 fluid ounces (1 cup) = 250 mL
12 fluid ounces (1 1/2 cups) = 375 mL
16 fluid ounces (2 cups) = 500 mL

WEIGHTS (mass)

1/2 ounce = 15 g
1 ounce = 30 g
3 ounces = 90 g
4 ounces = 120 g
8 ounces = 225 g
10 ounces = 285 g
12 ounces = 360 g
16 ounces = 1 pound = 450 g

DIMENSIONS

1/16 inch = 2 mm
1/8 inch = 3 mm
1/4 inch = 6 mm
1/2 inch = 1.5 cm
3/4 inch = 2 cm
1 inch = 2.5 cm

OVEN TEMPERATURES

250°F = 120°C
275°F = 140°C
300°F = 150°C
325°F = 160°C
350°F = 180°C
375°F = 190°C
400°F = 200°C
425°F = 220°C
450°F = 230°C

BAKING PAN SIZES

Utensil	Size in Inches/Quarts	Metric Volume	Size in Centimeters
Baking or Cake Pan (square or rectangular)	8×8×2	2 L	20×20×5
	9×9×2	2.5 L	23×23×5
	12×8×2	3 L	30×20×5
	13×9×2	3.5 L	33×23×5
Loaf Pan	8×4×3	1.5 L	20×10×7
	9×5×3	2 L	23×13×7
Round Layer Cake Pan	8×1½	1.2 L	20×4
	9×1½	1.5 L	23×4
Pie Plate	8×1¼	750 mL	20×3
	9×1¼	1 L	23×3
Baking Dish or Casserole	1 quart	1 L	—
	1½ quart	1.5 L	—
	2 quart	2 L	—